The Life of the Soul

The Wisdom of Julian of Norwich

*Translated by Edmund Colledge, O.S.A.,
and James Walsh, S.J.
Edited and with an introduction by Kathleen A. Walsh*

PAULIST PRESS
New York ◆ Mahwah, N.J.

Cover design by Tim McKeen. Cover photo by Don Kimball.

Copyright © 1996 by The Missionary Society of St. Paul the Apostle in the State of New York. The text of this volume is taken from *Julian of Norwich: Showings*, translated by Edmund Colledge, O.S.A., and James Walsh, S.J., copyright © 1978 by The Missionary Society of St. Paul the Apostle in the State of New York.

ISBN: 0-8091-3673-2

Published by Paulist Press
997 Macarthur Boulevard
Mahwah, New Jersey 07430

Printed and bound in the
United States of America

CONTENTS

INTRODUCTION

*I*n her one major work, *The Showings of the Love of God*, also referred to as *Revelations of Divine Love*, Julian of Norwich shares with us her remarkable insights into the soul and the spiritual life. While her mystical writing has become a famous and oft-read classic of spiritual literature, she herself remains a figure shrouded in mystery. From her *Showings*, we glean but a few historical details of her life, for it was not her purpose to speak of herself but to tell of the series of visions she received from God. Yet, despite the relative anonymity in which she is hidden, her deeply moving reflections have enabled us all to know this visionary and mystic in a way much more profound than any biographical details could convey. In her work we find a wisdom that has spoken to the hearts of spiritual seekers throughout the ages.

Although almost certainly not her real name, Julian was probably so called even during her life according to the custom that an anchoress adopt the name of the church with which she was associated. Julian lived in an anchorhold attached to the Church of St. Julian in

Norwich, England, although it is not clear exactly when she retired to the anchorhold. Restricted to the confines of her cell, her life in the anchorhold consisted of days spent in prayer and contemplation of God. The solitude of the anchoress, however, was not total. She had contact with a priest and with a trustworthy servant or two who attended to her domestic affairs. In addition, an anchoress was often sought out for guidance and consultation. Many anchorholds, including Julian's, possessed a small window allowing limited access to the outside world. Historical evidence suggests that Julian, having a reputation for holiness even during her lifetime, was often visited by those seeking her counsel and advice.

The testimony found in Julian's *Showings*, while divulging few details of her everyday routine, gives us insight into the more spiritual aspects of her life. She relates in the opening chapters that when she was younger she had prayed for three things specifically. The first prayer was for a vision of Christ's passion so that she could know better his sufferings and "might have suffered with him as others did who loved him." The second request was for a severe illness that would bring her near death and break within her any attachment toward earthly things, enabling her to cultivate a greater awareness of lasting values and to increase her focus on Christ. Lastly, she prayed for three "wounds" or gifts, "the wound of true contrition, the wound of loving compassion and the wound of longing with my will for God."

The request for these three wounds stemmed from her desire to connect in a truly personal way with Christ's passion. The desire for contrition was not just a prayer for true repentance for sin, but also for an internal shift away from self-centeredness toward God. In asking for the wound of compassion, Julian desired true care and concern for the other without allowing the preoccupations of personal concerns to intrude. Finally, the wound of longing for God was a request for a directness of purpose in following God so that beyond the vagaries of emotions and feelings, dry spells and periods rich in prayer, she might ever have the strong and abiding desire for God.

Of these three requests, the first two she had prayed for conditionally, seeking their fulfillment only if that be God's will for her. They passed from her mind during the course of time. The desire for a vision and for a severe illness, however, was unexpectedly fulfilled in

May of 1373 when she was "thirty and a half years old." At that time she contracted a serious sickness, and death appeared imminent. She was given last rites and a crucifix was held before her so that she might reflect upon Christ crucified as she met her end. Instead of death, however, she felt a sudden relief of her pain and received a series of fifteen visions, with a sixteenth coming the following day.

Julian wrote down an initial version of the visions in what is referred to as the Short Text. She spent the next twenty years revisiting and reflecting on her experience, then composed a later manuscript version known as the Long Text. Both versions begin with the circumstances of Julian's severe illness and the contents of each vision, but the Long Text adds a considerable amount of theological commentary and spiritual discussion about such questions as the nature of the soul, the relationship between God and humanity, the existence of sin, the meaning of suffering, and the inner life of the Trinity.

Although Julian is often noted for her discussion of the motherhood of God, another striking aspect of *Showings*, one explored in the following selections from that work, is her deep understanding of the human person. Her anthropology is rooted in the understanding that, created in God's image, we reflect the wholeness and goodness of the divine. Julian even describes the soul as "a created trinity" and "God's dwelling place." Her understanding of the life of the soul centers around the basic premise of our goodness and yet our basic alienation from God, which corresponds to her discussion of the soul in terms of substance and sensuality. [1]

Substance, the "higher" part, is the essence of our humanity as created by God. We exist only in God, who is the source and ground of all being. Sensuality, the "lower" part of the soul, is that which comprises our freedom and independence and includes our physical and psychological natures as human beings. This construct does not in any way refer to a schism between body and soul or a negativity about the body. Julian had too great an appreciation for the goodness of creation for that. Rather, both aspects belong to the soul. Both, too, are present in Jesus Christ, although he

[1] For a further discussion of substance and sensuality, see Chapter 8, "Creation and Asceticism: Expressions of Love," especially pp. 137–149, in *Julian of Norwich: Mystic and Theologian* by Grace Jantzen (Paulist Press, 1988).

shares substance with the Father by virtue of being begotten, while we have a share by virtue of our creation in God.

Julian notes that these two parts of the soul are often out of sync. Our substance, by virtue of our creation, is united always with God. But our sensuality is often mired in patterns of thought and behavior that draw us away from our essence and into self-centeredness. Our feelings of alienation and brokenness are the direct result of the internal division between our "godly will," our abiding unity in substance with God, and our sensuality. We are like a house divided, for we often attempt to find fulfillment in earthly things when our deepest longings for wholeness can only be fulfilled by union in God. "This is the reason," Julian writes, "why no soul is at rest until it has despised as nothing all things which are created."

This lack of integration at the heart of the human condition is the basic human sin, or original sin. Individual sins are at their root an outgrowth from the basic sinful condition in which we find ourselves. This fundamental brokenness and fragmentation is a common heritage to which each person contributes and by which each is affected. And yet sin, according to

Julian, is nothing. It has "no kind of substance, no share in being, nor can it be recognized except by the pain caused by it." This does not mean sin is non-existent, but rather that it has no substance, for God is the source of all substance and thus all substance is good. Evil and sin, therefore, are a negation of goodness and being. They are not the ultimate fact about ourselves and our existence.

The lack of integration between substance and sensuality results in a conflict between our godly will, "which never assents to sin and never will," and our sensuality, which by virtue of our freedom and our choices is pulled into sins and moral failures. Our unity with God is, to Julian, a sign that we are fundamentally good, even if not on a conscious level, yet much of her work explores why our souls became so fragmented, why sin came into existence and why it continues. According to Julian, sin is the basic cause of all human suffering, and this fundamental alienation of the individual from God manifests itself in our relationship to others. Like a wound at the very heart of being, we suffer from it and inflict suffering on others because of it.

The pain and despair of the soul come not as a

result of God's blame, for in everything God sees our fundamental unity with him and our utter worthiness for love. Rather, it derives from our inability to see ourselves as God sees us, a blindness that is at heart a result of our fallen human condition. As Julian puts it, "all our travail is because love is lacking on our side," for God looks upon us with pity, understanding that because of our confusion and internal division we do not fully know ourselves or our desire for goodness and for him. While Julian has no complete answer to the problem of suffering and sin, she trusts in a vision she received that all will be well, that God will accomplish a remarkable deed in which all things will be healed. This is not meant as a trivialization of our suffering, but as a consolation.

Along with her belief that we will be delivered from our suffering, Julian holds that our suffering will be worth it.[2] She does not mean that gratuitous suffering is positive, but that the joys we will receive will make

---

[2] Jantzen has a fuller discussion of both Julian's idea that "all will be well" and that sin will be rewarded in Chapter 9, "Sin and Suffering," especially pp. 173–190.

suffering worthwhile. In essence, rather than speak of rewards for good deeds, Julian speaks of reward from sin, believing that "just as there is indeed a corresponding pain for every sin, just so love gives to the soul a bliss for every sin." If indeed suffering is to be rewarded, then original sin, our greatest pain and the cause of all the rest of our suffering, must certainly find heavenly recompense. This reward must be intrinsic to the sin in some way, so that the sin itself is necessary for its bestowal.

Julian holds that it is because of this fragmentation of the human person which results from sin that the "wounds" of contrition, compassion, and longing for God can be developed. Julian refers to these three means as "medicines." Through our sorrow and humble seeking we open ourselves more to a true union in God and begin the process of healing our badly divided soul. The wound by which we were so grievously hurt has been transformed into the wounds that lead us into further integration in ourselves and in God. This is what Julian means when she speaks of wounds being turned into honors. She never implies that this transformation is something that we will recognize in this life or fully comprehend. Yet her under-

9

standing of the reward consoles her with its powerful claim that sin is not the final word about human nature, just as death was not the final word about Christ.

From her initial recollection of the gift of Christ's passion, Julian came to a greater understanding of the basic brokenness of human life, our deep need for love, and the sense of inner worth that comes from knowing we are of God. The selections from her *Showings* included here present some of her tender, moving reflections on the life of the soul which bespeak an experience of and exploration into the struggles and questions that have remained universal in the spiritual life. Although space does not permit a full exploration of her visions or of her expanded commentary, these excerpts from the Long Text give the reader insight into the spiritual riches bestowed initially on Julian which have since become the treasure of generations of Christian readers.

FROM THE FIRST REVELATION

"...no soul is at rest until it has despised as nothing all things which are created."

Our good Lord showed a spiritual sight of his familiar love. I saw that he is to us everything which is good and comforting for our help. He is our clothing, who wraps and enfolds us for love, embraces us and shelters us, surrounds us for his love, which is so tender that he may never desert us. And so in this sight I saw that he is everything which is good, as I understand.

And in this he showed me something small, no bigger than a hazelnut, lying in the palm of my hand, as it seemed to me, and it was as round as a ball. I looked at it with the eye of my understanding and thought: What can this be? I was amazed that it could last, for I thought that because of its littleness it would suddenly have fallen into nothing. And I was answered in my understanding: It lasts and always will, because God loves it; and thus everything has being through the love of God.

In this little thing I saw three properties. The first is that God made it, the second is that God loves it, the third is that God preserves it. But what did I see in it? It is that God is the Creator and the protector and the lover. For until I am substantially united to him, I can never have perfect rest or true happiness, until, that is, I am so attached to him that there can be no created thing between my God and me.

This little thing which is created seemed to me as if it could have fallen into nothing because of its littleness. We need to have knowledge of this, so that we may delight in despising as nothing everything created, so as to love and have uncreated God. For this is the reason why our hearts and souls are not in perfect ease, because here we seek rest in this thing which is so little, in which there is no rest, and we do not know our God who is almighty, all wise and all good, for he is true rest. God wishes to be known, and it pleases him that we should rest in him; for everything which is beneath him is not sufficient for us. And this is the reason why no soul is at rest until it has despised as nothing all things which are created. When it by its will has become nothing for love, to have him who is everything, then is it able to receive spiritual rest.

And also our good Lord revealed that it is very greatly pleasing to him that a simple soul should come naked, openly and familiarly. For this is the loving yearning of the soul through the touch of the Holy Spirit, from the understanding which I have in this revelation: God, of your goodness give me yourself, for you are enough for me, and I can ask for nothing which is less which can pay you full worship. And if I ask anything which is less, always I am in want; but only in you do I have everything.

And these words of the goodness of God are very dear to the soul, and very close to touching our Lord's will, for his goodness fills all his creatures and all his blessed works full, and endlessly overflows in them. For he is everlastingness, and he made us only for himself, and restored us by his precious Passion and always preserves us in his blessed love; and all this is of his goodness.

◆

"For he does not despise what he has made, nor does he disdain to serve us in the simplest natural functions of our body, for love of the soul which he created in his own likeness."

A man walks upright, and the food in his body is shut in as if in a well-made purse. When the time of his necessity comes, the purse is opened and then shut again, in most seemly fashion. And it is God who does this, as it is shown when he says that he comes down to us in our humblest needs. For he does not despise what he has made, nor does he disdain to serve us in the simplest natural functions of our body, for love of the soul which he created in his own likeness. For as the body is clad in the cloth, and the flesh in the skin, and the bones in the flesh, and the heart in the trunk, so are we, soul and body, clad and enclosed in the goodness of God. Yes, and more closely, for all these vanish and waste away; the goodness of God is always complete, and closer to us, beyond any comparison. For truly our lover desires the soul to adhere to him with all its power, and us always to adhere to his goodness. For of all the things that the heart can think, this pleases God most and soonest profits the soul. For it is so preciously loved by him who is highest that this surpasses the knowledge of all created beings. That is to say, there is no created being who can know how much and how sweetly and how tenderly the Creator loves us. And therefore we can with his grace and his help persevere in spiritual contemplation, with endless wonder at this high, surpassing, immeasurable love which our Lord in his goodness has for us; and therefore we may with reverence ask from our lover all that we will, for our natural will is to have God, and God's good will is to have us, and we can never stop willing or loving until we possess him in the fulness of joy. And there we can will no more, for it is his will that we be occupied in knowing and loving until the time comes that we shall be filled full in heaven.

And therefore this lesson of love was revealed, with all that follows, as you will see, for the strength and foundation of everything was revealed in the first vision. For of all things, contemplating and loving the Creator makes the soul to seem less in its own sight, and fills it full with reverent fear and true meekness, and with much love for its fellow Christians.

FROM THE THIRD REVELATION

"...our Lord wants to have the soul truly converted to contemplation of him and of all his works in general. For they are most good, and all his judgments are easy and sweet, bringing to great rest the soul which is converted from contemplating men's blind judgments to the judgments, lovely and sweet, of our Lord God."

*A*nd after this I saw God in an instant of time, that is to say in my understanding, by which vision I saw that he is present in all things. I contemplated it carefully, seeing and recognizing through it that he does everything which is done. I marvelled at that vision with a gentle fear, and I thought: What is sin? For I saw truly that God does everything, however, small it may be, and that nothing is done by chance, but all by God's prescient wisdom. If it seem chance in man's sight, our blindness and lack of prescience is the reason. For those things which are in God's prescient wisdom since before time, which duly and to his glory he always guides to their best conclusion, as things come about, come suddenly upon us when we are ignorant; and so through our blindness and our lack of prescience we say that these things are by chance.

So I understood in this revelation of love, for I know well that in our Lord's sight there is no chance; and therefore I was compelled to admit that everything which is done is well done, for our Lord God does everything. For at this time the work of creatures was not revealed, but the work of our Lord God in creatures; for he is at the centre of everything, and he does everything. And I was certain that he does no sin; and here I was certain that sin is no deed, for in all this sin was not shown to me. And I did not wish to go on wondering about this, but I contemplated our Lord and waited for what he would show. And thus the rightfulness of God's dealing was shown to the soul, as well as could be in that time. Rightfulness has two fine qualities: It is right and it is full. And so are all the works of our Lord, and they lack no operation of mercy or of grace, for they are all rightful and nothing whatever is lacking in them....

This vision was revealed to my understanding, for our Lord wants to have the soul truly converted to contemplation of him and of all his works in general. For they are most good, and all his judgments are easy and sweet, bringing to great rest the soul which is converted from contemplating men's blind judgments to the judgments, lovely and sweet, of our Lord God. For a man regards some deeds as well done and some as evil, and our Lord does not regard them so, for everything which exists in nature is of God's creation, so that everything which is done has the property of being of God's doing. For it is easy to understand that the best of deeds is well done; and the smallest of deeds which is done is as well done as the best and the greatest, and they all have the property and the order ordained for them as our Lord had ordained, without beginning, for no one does but he.

I saw most truly that he never changed his purpose in any kind of thing, nor ever will eternally. For there was nothing unknown to him in his just ordinance before time began, and therefore all things were set in order, before anything was made, as it would endure eternally. And no kind of thing will fail in that respect, for he has made everything totally good.

And therefore the blessed Trinity is always wholly pleased with all its works; and God revealed all this most blessedly, as though to say: See, I am God. See, I am in all things. See, I do all things. See, I never remove my hands from my works, nor ever shall without end. See, I guide all things to the end that I ordain them for, before time began, with the same power and wisdom and love with which I made them; how should anything be amiss? So was the soul examined, powerfully, wisely and lovingly, in this vision. Then I saw truly that I must agree, with great reverence and joy in God.

FROM THE TWELFTH REVELATION

"...our soul will never have rest till it comes into him, acknowledging that he is full of joy, familiar and courteous and blissful and true life."

And after this our Lord showed himself to me, and he appeared to me more glorified than I had seen him before, in which I was taught that our soul will never have rest till it comes into him, acknowledging that he is full of joy, familiar and courteous and blissful and true life. Again and again our Lord said: I am he, I am he, I am he who is highest. I am he whom you love. I am he in whom you delight. I am he whom you serve. I am he for whom you long. I am he whom you desire. I am he whom you intend. I am he who is all. I am he whom Holy Church preaches and teaches to you. I am he who showed himself before to you. The number of the words surpasses my intelligence and my understanding and all my powers, for they were the most exalted, as I see it, for in them is comprehended I cannot tell what; but the joy which I saw when they were revealed surpasses all that the heart can think or the soul may desire. And therefore these words are not explained here, but let every man accept them as our Lord intended them, according to the grace God gives him in understanding and love.

FROM THE THIRTEENTH REVELATION

"...all will be well, and all will be well, and every kind of thing will be well."

*A*nd after this our Lord brought to my mind the longing that I had for him before, and I saw that nothing hindered me but sin, and I saw that this is true of us all in general, and it seemed to me that if there had been no sin, we should all have been pure and as like our Lord as he created us. And so in my folly before this time I often wondered why, through the great prescient wisdom of God, the beginning of sin was not prevented. For then it seemed to me that all would have been well.

The impulse to think this was greatly to be shunned; and nevertheless I mourned and sorrowed on this account, unreasonably, lacking discretion. But Jesus, who in this vision informed me about everything needful to me, answered with these words and said: Sin is necessary, but all will be well, and all will be well, and every kind of thing will be well. In this naked word 'sin,' our Lord brought generally to my mind all which is not good, and the shameful contempt and the direst tribulation which he endured for us in this life, and his death and all his pains, and the passions, spiritual and bodily, of all his creatures. For we are all in part troubled, and we shall be troubled, following our master Jesus until we are fully purged of our mortal flesh and all our inward affections which are not very good.

And with the beholding of this, with all the pains that ever were or ever will be, I understood Christ's Passion for the greatest and surpassing pain. And yet this was shown to me in an instant, and it quickly turned into consolation. For our good Lord would not have the soul frightened by this ugly sight. But I did not see sin, for I believe that it has no kind of substance, no share in being, nor can it be recognized except by the pain caused by it. And it seems to me that this pain is something for a time, for it purges and makes us know ourselves and ask for mercy; for the Passion of our Lord is comfort to us against all this, and that is his blessed will. And because of the tender love which our good Lord has for all who will be saved, he comforts readily and sweetly, meaning this: It is true that sin is the cause of all this pain, but all will be well, and every kind of thing will be well.

These words were revealed most tenderly, showing no kind of blame to me or to anyone who will be saved. So it would be most unkind of me to blame God or marvel at him on account of my sins, since he does not blame me for sin.

And in these same words I saw hidden in God an exalted and wonderful mystery, which he will make plain and we shall know in heaven. In this knowledge we shall truly see the cause why he allowed sin to come, and in this sight we shall rejoice forever.

So I saw how Christ has compassion on us because of sin; and just as I was before filled full of pain and compassion on account of Christ's Passion, so I was now in part filled with compassion for all my fellow Christians, because he loves very dearly the people who will be saved, that is to say God's servants. Holy Church will be shaken in sorrow and anguish and tribulation in this world as men shake a cloth in the wind; and in this matter our Lord answered, revealing in this way: Ah, I shall turn this into a great thing, of endless honour and everlasting joy, in heaven. Yes, I even saw that our Lord rejoices with pity and compassion over the tribulations of his servants; and he imposes on every person whom he loves, to bring him to his bliss, something that is no defect in his sight, through which souls are humiliated and despised in this world, scorned and mocked and rejected. And he does this to prevent the harm which they might have from the pomps and the pride and the vainglory of this wretched life, and to prepare their way to come to heaven, into endless, everlasting bliss. For he says: I shall completely break down in you your empty affections and your vicious pride, and then I shall gather you and make you meek and mild, pure and holy through union with me.

And then I saw that every natural compassion which one has for one's fellow Christians in love is Christ in us, and that every kind of self-humiliation which he manifested in his Passion was manifested again in this compassion, in which there were two different understandings of our Lord's intention. One was the bliss that we are brought to, in which he wants us to rejoice. The other is for consolation in our pain, for he wants us to know that it will all be turned to our honour and profit by the power of his Passion, and to know that we suffered in no way alone, but together with him, and to see in him our foundation. And he wants us to see that his pains and his tribulation exceed all that we may suffer so far that it cannot be comprehended in full. And if we well contemplate his will in this, it keeps us from lamenting and despairing as we experience our pains; and if we see truly that our sins deserve them, still his love excuses us. And of his great courtesy he puts away all our blame, and regards us with pity and compassion as innocent and guiltless children.

But in this I stood, contemplating it generally, darkly and mournfully, saying in intention to our Lord with very great fear: Ah, good Lord, how could all things be well, because of the great harm which has come through sin to your creatures? And here I wished, so far as I dared, for some plainer explanation through which I might be at ease about this matter. And to this our blessed Lord answered, very meekly and with a most loving manner, and he showed that Adam's sin was the greatest harm ever done or ever to be done until the end of the world. And he also showed me that this is plainly known to all Holy Church upon earth.

Furthermore, he taught that I should contemplate the glorious atonement, for this atoning is more pleasing to the blessed divinity and more honourable for man's salvation, without comparison, than ever

Adam's sin was harmful. So then this is our blessed Lord's intention, and in this teaching we should pay heed to this: For since I have set right the greatest of harms, then it is my will that you should know through this that I shall set right everything which is less.

He gave understanding of two portions. One portion is our saviour and our salvation. This blessed portion is open, clear, fair and bright and plentiful, for all men who are of good will are comprehended in this portion. We are bound to this by God, and drawn and counselled and taught, inwardly by the Holy Spirit, and outwardly through the same grace by Holy Church. Our Lord wants us to be occupied in this, rejoicing in him, for he rejoices in us. And the more plentifully we accept from this with reverence and humility, the more do we deserve thanks from him, and the more profit do we win for ourselves. And so we may see and rejoice that our portion is our Lord.

The other portion is hidden from us and closed, that is to say all which is additional to our salvation; for this is our Lord's privy counsel, and it is fitting to God's royal dominion to keep his privy counsel in peace, and it is fitting to his servants out of obedience and respect not to wish to know his counsel.

Our Lord has pity and compassion on us because some creatures occupy themselves so much in this; and I am sure that if we knew how greatly we should please him and solace ourselves by leaving it alone, we should do so. The saints in heaven, they wish to know nothing but what our Lord wishes them to know, and furthermore their love and their desire are governed according to our Lord's will; and we should do this, so that our will resembles theirs. Then we shall not wish or desire anything but the will of our Lord, as they do, for we are all one in God's intention.

And in this I was taught that we shall rejoice only our blessed saviour Jesus, and trust in him for everything.

And so our good Lord answered to all the questions and doubts which I could raise, saying most comfortingly: I may make all things well, and I can make all things well, and I shall make all things well, and I will make all things well; and you will see yourself that every kind of thing will be well. When he says 'I may,' I understand this to apply to the Father; and when he says 'I can,' I understand it for the Son; and when he says 'I will,' I understand it for the Holy Spirit; and when he says 'I shall,' I understand it for the unity of the blessed Trinity, three persons and one truth; and when he says 'You will see yourself,' I understand it for the union of all men who will be saved in the blessed Trinity.

And in these five words God wishes us to be enclosed in rest and in peace. And so Christ's spiritual thirst will have an end. For this is Christ's spiritual thirst, his longing in love, which persists and always will until we see him on the day of judgment, for we who shall be saved and shall be Christ's joy and bliss are still here, and some are yet to come, and so will some be until that day. Therefore this is his thirst and his longing in love for us, to gather us all here into him, to our endless joy, as I see it. For we are not now so wholly in him as we then shall be....

On one occasion our good Lord said: Every kind of thing will be well, and on another occasion he said: You will see yourself that every kind of thing will be well. And from these two the soul gained different kinds of understanding. One was this: that he wants us to know that he takes heed not only of things which are noble and great, but also of those which are little and small, of humble men and simple, of this man and that man. And this is what he means when he says:

Every kind of thing will be well. For he wants us to know that the smallest thing will not be forgotten. Another understanding is this: that there are many deeds which in our eyes are so evilly done and lead to such great harms that it seems to us impossible that any good result could ever come of them. And we contemplate this and sorrow and mourn for it so that we cannot rest in the blessed contemplation of God as we ought to do. And the cause is this: that the reason which we use is now so blind, so abject and so stupid that we cannot recognize God's exalted, wonderful wisdom, or the power and the goodness of the blessed Trinity. And this is his intention when he says: You will see yourself that every kind of things will be well, as if he said: Accept it now in faith and trust, and in the very end you will see truly, in fulness of joy.

And so in the same five words said before: I may make all things well, I understand a powerful comfort from all the works of our Lord God which are still to come.

There is a deed which the blessed Trinity will perform on the last day, as I see it, and what the deed will be and how it will be performed is unknown to every creature who is inferior to Christ, and it will be until the deed is done. The goodness and the love of our Lord God want us to know that this will be, and his power and his wisdom, through the same love, want to conceal it and hide it from us, what it will be and how it will be done. And the cause why he wants us to know it like this is because he wants us to be at ease in our souls and at peace in love, disregarding every disturbance which could hinder our true rejoicing in him.

This is the great deed ordained by our Lord God from without beginning, treasured and hidden in his blessed breast, known only to himself, through which deed he will make all things well. For just as the blessed Trinity created all things from nothing, just so will the same blessed Trinity make everything well which is not well. And I marvelled greatly at this sight, and contemplated our faith, with this in my mind: Our faith is founded on God's word, and it belongs to our faith that we believe that God's word will be preserved in all things. And one article of our faith is that many creatures will be damned, such as the angels who fell out of heaven because of pride, who now are devils, and many men upon earth who die out of the faith of Holy Church, that is to say those who are pagans and many who have received baptism and who live unchristian lives and so die out of God's love. All these will be eternally condemned to hell, as Holy Church teaches me to believe.

And all this being so, it seemed to me that it was impossible that every kind of thing should be well, as our Lord revealed at this time. And to this I had no other answer as a revelation from our Lord except this: What is impossible to you is not impossible to me. I shall preserve my word in everything, and I shall make everything well. And in this I was taught by the grace of God that I ought to keep myself steadfastly in the faith, as I had understood before, and that at the same time I should stand firm and believe firmly that every kind of thing will be well, as our Lord revealed at that same time. For this is the great deed which our Lord will do, and in this deed he will preserve his word in everything. And he will make well all which is not well. But what the deed will be and how it will be done, there is no creature who is inferior to Christ who knows it, or will know it until it has been done, according to the understanding which I received of our Lord's meaning at this time.

◆

"And God showed that sin will be no shame, but honour to man, for just as there is indeed a corresponding pain for every sin, just so loves gives to the same soul a bliss for every sin."

God brought to mind that I should sin; and because of the delight that I had in contemplating him, I did not at once pay attention to that revelation. And our Lord very mercifully waited, and gave me grace to attend; and I applied this revelation particularly to myself. But by all the consolations of grace which follow, as you will see, I was taught to apply it to all my fellow Christians, to all in general and not to any in particular.

Though our Lord revealed to me that I should sin, by me is understood everyone. And in this I conceived a gentle fear, and in answer to this our Lord said: I protect you very safely. This word was said with more love and assurance of protection for my soul than I can or may tell. For just as it was first revealed to me that I should sin, so was consolation revealed—assurance of protection for all my fellow Christians. What can make me love my fellow Christians more than to see in God that he loves all who will be saved, all of them as it were one soul? For in every soul which will be saved there is a godly will which never assents to sin and never will. Just as there is an animal will in the lower part which cannot will any good, so there is a godly will in the higher part, which will is so good that it cannot ever will any evil, but always good. And therefore we are they whom he loves, and eternally we do what he delights in. And our Lord revealed this to me in the completeness of his love, that we are standing in his sight, yes, that he loves us now whilst we are here as well as he will when we are there, before his blessed face; but all our travail is because love is lacking on our side.

And God showed that sin will be no shame, but honour to man, for just as there is indeed a corresponding pain for every sin, just so love gives to the same soul a bliss for every sin. Just as various sins are punished with various pains, the more grievous are the sins, so will they be rewarded with various joys in heaven to reward the victories over them, to the degree in which the sin may have been painful and sorrowful to the soul on earth. For the soul which will come to heaven is so precious to God, and its place there so honourable, that God's goodness never suffers the soul to sin finally which will come there. But who are the sinners who will be so rewarded is known to Holy Church, on earth and also in heaven, by their surpassing honours. For in this sight my understanding was lifted up into heaven; and then God brought joyfully to my mind David and innumerable others with him in the Old Law; and in the New Law he brought to my mind first Magdalen, Peter and Paul, Thomas of India, St. John of Beverly and others too without number; how they and their sins are known to the Church on earth, and this is no shame to them, but everything is turned to their honour. And therefore our courteous Lord gives a partial revelation about them here of what is there in fulness; for there the mark of sin is turned to honour....

◆

"By contrition we are made clean, by compassion we are made ready, and by true longing for God we are made worthy. These are three means, as I understand, through which all souls come to heaven, those, that is to say, who have been sinners on earth and will be saved. For every sinful soul must be healed by these medicines."

Sin is the sharpest scourge with which any chosen soul can be struck, which scourge belabours man or woman, and breaks a man, and purges him in his own sight so much that at times he thinks himself that he is not fit for anything but as it were to sink into hell, until contrition seizes him by the inspiration of the Holy Spirit and turns bitterness into hope of God's mercy. And then the wounds begin to heal and the soul to revive, restored to the life of Holy Church. The Holy Spirit leads him to confession, willing to reveal his sins, nakedly and truthfully, with great sorrow and great shame that he has so befouled God's fair image. Then he accepts the penance for every sin imposed by his confessor, for this is established in Holy Church by the teaching of the Holy Spirit, and this is one meekness which greatly pleases God; and he also meekly accepts bodily sickness sent by God, and sorrows and outward shames, with the reproofs and contempt of the world and with all kinds of affliction and temptations into which we are cast, spiritually and bodily.

Our good Lord protects us with the greatest of loving care when it seems to us that we are almost forsaken and abandoned because of our sins and because we see that we have deserved it. And because of the meekness that we obtain from this, we are raised very high in God's sight by his grace. And also God in his special grace visits whom he will with such great contrition, and also with compassion and true longing for him, that they are suddenly delivered from sin and from pain, and taken up into bliss and made equal with the saints. By contrition we are made clean, by compassion we are made ready, and by true longing for God we are made worthy. These are three means, as I understand, through which all souls come to heaven, those, that is to say, who have been sinners on earth and will be saved.

For every sinful soul must be healed by these medicines. Though he be healed, his wounds are not seen by God as wounds but as honours. And as we are punished here with sorrow and penance, in contrary fashion we shall be rewarded in heaven by the courteous love of our almighty God, who does not wish anyone who comes there to lose his labours in any degree. For he regards sin as sorrow and pains for his lovers, to whom for love he assigns no blame.

The reward which we shall receive will not be small, but it will be great, glorious and honourable. And so all shame will be turned into honour and joy.

For our courteous Lord does not want his servants to despair because they fall often and grievously; for our falling does not hinder him in loving us. Peace and love are always in us, living and working, but we are not always in peace and in love; but he wants us so to take heed that he is the foundation of our whole life in love, and furthermore that he is our everlasting protector, and mightily defends us against all our enemies, who are very cruel and very fierce towards us, and so our need is great, the more so because by our falling we give them occasion.

And this is a supreme friendship of our courteous Lord, that he protects us so tenderly whilst we are in our sins; and furthermore he touches us most secretly, and shows us our sins by the sweet light of mercy and grace. But when we see ourselves so foul, then we believe that God may be angry with us because of our sins. Then we are moved by the Holy Spirit through contrition to prayer, and we desire with all our might an amendment of ourselves to appease God's anger, until the time that we find rest of soul and ease of conscience. And then we hope that God has forgiven us our sin; and this is true. And then our courteous Lord shows himself to the soul, happily and with the gladdest countenance, welcoming it as a friend, as if it had been in pain and in prison, saying: My dear darling, I am glad that you have come to me in all your woe. I have always been with you, and now you see me loving, and we are made one in bliss.

So sins are forgiven by grace and mercy, and our soul is honourably received in joy, as it will be when it comes into heaven, as often as it comes by the operation of grace of the Holy Spirit and the power of Christ's Passion.

Here I truly understood that every kind of thing is made available to us by God's great goodness, so much so that when we ourselves are at peace and in charity we are truly safe. But because we cannot have this completely whilst we are here, therefore it is fitting for us to live always in sweet prayer and in loving longing with our Lord Jesus. For he always longs to bring us to the fulness of joy,...where he reveals his spiritual thirst. But now, because of all this spiritual consolation which has been described, if any man or woman be moved by folly to say or to think 'If this be true, then it would be well to sin so as to have the greater reward, or else to think sin less important,' beware of this impulse, for truly, should it come, it is untrue and from the fiend.

For the same true love which touches us all by its blessed strength, that same blessed love teaches us that we must hate sin only because of love. And I am sure by what I feel that the more that each loving soul sees this in the courteous love of our Lord God, the greater is his hatred of sinning and the more he is ashamed. For if it were laid in front of us, all the pain there is in hell and in purgatory and on earth, death and all the rest, we should choose all that pain rather than sin. For sin is so vile and so much to be hated that it can be compared with no pain which is not itself sin. And no more cruel hell than sin was revealed to me, for a loving soul hates no pain but sin; for everything is good except sin, and nothing is evil except sin. And when by the operation of mercy and grace we set our intention on mercy and grace, we are made all fair and spotless.

And God is as willing as he is powerful and wise to save man. And Christ himself is the foundation of all the laws of Christian men, and he taught us to do good in return for evil. Here we may see that he is himself this love, and does to us as he teaches us to do; for he wishes us to be like him in undiminished, everlasting love towards ourselves and our fellow Christians. No more than his love towards us is withdrawn because of our sin does he wish our love to be withdrawn from ourselves or from our fellow Christians; but we must unreservedly hate sin and endlessly love the soul as God loves it. Then we should hate sin just as God hates it, and love the soul as God loves it. For these words which God said are an endless strength: I protect you most truly.

FROM THE FOURTEENTH REVELATION

"Prayer unites the soul to God, for though the soul may be always like God in nature and in substance restored by grace, it is often unlike him in condition, through sin on man's part. Then prayer is a witness that the soul wills as God wills, and it eases the conscience and fits man for grace."

After this our Lord revealed about prayer, in which revelation I saw two conditions in our Lord's intention. One is rightful prayer; the other is confident trust. But still our trust is often not complete, because we are not sure that God hears us, as we think, because of our unworthiness and because we are feeling nothing at all; for often we are as barren and dry after our prayers as we were before. And thus when we feel so, it is our folly which is the cause of our weakness, for I have experienced this in myself. And our Lord brought all this suddenly to my mind, and revealed these words and said: I am the ground of your beseeching. First, it is my will that you should have it, and then I make you to wish it, and then I make you to beseech it. If you beseech it, how could it be that you would not have what you beseech? And so in the first reason and in the three that follow, our Lord reveals a great strengthening, as can be seen in the same words.

And in the first reason, where he says: if you beseech, he shows his great delight, and the everlasting reward that he will give us for our beseeching. And in the second reason, where he says: How could it be? this was said as an impossibility; for it is the most impossible that that may be that we should seek mercy and grace and not have it. For everything which our good Lord makes us to beseech he himself has ordained for us from all eternity. So here we may see that our beseeching is not the cause of the goodness and grace which he gives us, but his own goodness. And that he truly revealed in all these sweet words, where he says: I am the foundation. And our good Lord wants this to be known by his lovers on earth. And the more that we know this, the more shall we beseech, if it be wisely accepted, and this is our Lord's intention.

Beseeching is a true and gracious, enduring will of the soul, united and joined to our Lord's will by the sweet, secret operation of the Holy Spirit. Our Lord himself is the first receiver of our prayer, as I see it, and he accepts it most thankfully, and greatly rejoicing he sends it up above, and puts it in a treasure-house where it will never perish. It is there before God with all his holy saints, continually received, always furthering our needs. And when we shall receive our bliss, it will be given to us as a measure of joy, with endless, honourable thanks from him.

Our Lord is most glad and joyful because of our prayer; and he expects it, and he wants to have it, for with his grace it makes us like to himself in condition as we are in nature, and such is his blessed will. For he says: Pray wholeheartedly, though it seems to you that this has no savour for you; still it is profitable enough, though you may not feel that. Pray whole-heartedly, though you may feel nothing, though you may see nothing, yes, though you think that you could not, for in dryness and in barrenness, in sick-ness and weakness, then is your prayer most pleasing to me, though you think it almost tasteless to you. And so is all your living prayer in my sight.

Because of the reward and the endless thanks that he will give us there, because he covets to have us praying continually in his sight, God accepts the good will and the labour of his servants, however we may feel, and therefore it pleases him that we work in prayer and in good living by his help and his grace, reasonably and with discretion, preserving our powers for him until we have in the fulness of joy him whom we seek, who is Jesus....

Thanksgiving also belongs to prayer. Thanksgiving is a true inward acknowledgment, we applying ourselves with great reverence and loving fear and with all our powers to the work that our Lord moved us to, rejoicing and giving thanks inwardly. And sometimes the soul is so full of this that it breaks out in words and says: Good Lord, great thanks, blessed may you be. And sometimes the heart is dry and feels nothing, or else, by the temptation of our enemy, reason and grace drive the soul to implore our Lord with words, recounting his blessed Passion and his great goodness. And so the power of our Lord's word enters the soul and enlivens the heart and it begins by his grace faithful exercise, and makes the soul to pray most blessedly, and truly to rejoice in our Lord. This is a most loving thanksgiving in his sight....

Prayer unites the soul to God, for though the soul may be always like God in nature and in substance restored by grace, it is often unlike him in condition, through sin on man's part. Then prayer is a witness that the soul wills as God wills, and it eases the conscience and fits man for grace. And so he teaches us to pray and to have firm trust that we shall have it; for he beholds us in love, and wants to make us partners in his good will and work. And so he moves us to pray for what it pleases him to do, and for this prayer and good desire which come to us by his gift he will repay us, and give us eternal reward. And this was revealed to me when he said: If you beseech it.

In this saying God showed such great pleasure and such great delight, as though he were much beholden to us for each good deed that we do; and yet it is he who does it.

Therefore we pray to him urgently that he may do what is pleasing to him, as if he were to say: How could you please me more than by entreating me, urgently, wisely and sincerely, to do the thing that I want to have done? And so the soul by prayer is made of one accord with God.

But when our courteous Lord of his special grace shows himself to our soul, we have what we desire, and then for that time we do not see what more we should pray for, but all our intention and all our powers are wholly directed to contemplating him. And as I see it, this is an exalted and imperceptible prayer; for the whole reason why we pray is to be united into the vision and contemplation of him to whom we pray, wonderfully rejoicing with reverent fear, and with so much sweetness and delight in him that we cannot pray at all except as he moves us at the time.

And well I know that the more the soul sees of God, the more she desires him by grace; but when we do not see him so, then we feel need and reason to pray, because we are failing and unfit for Jesus. For when a soul is tempted, troubled and left to herself in her unrest, that is the time for her to pray and to make herself supple and obedient to God. But he [that is, the soul] by no kind of prayer makes God supple to him; for God's love does not change. And so I saw that when we see the need for us to pray, then our Lord God is following us, helping our desire. And when we by his special grace behold him plainly, seeing no other, we then necessarily follow him, and he draws us to him by love. For I saw and felt that his wonderful and total goodness fulfils all our powers; and with that I saw that his continual working in every kind of thing is done so divinely, so wisely and so powerfully that it surpasses all our imagining and everything that we can understand or think. And then we can do no more than contemplate him and rejoice, with a great and compelling desire to be wholly united into him, and attend to his motion and rejoice in his love and delight in his goodness.

And so we shall by his sweet grace in our own meek continual prayer come into him now in this life by many secret touchings of sweet spiritual sights and feelings, measured out to us as our simplicity may bear it. And this is done and will be done by the grace of the Holy Spirit, until the day that we die, still longing for love. And then we shall all come into our Lord, knowing ourselves clearly and wholly possessing God, and we shall all be endlessly hidden in God, truly seeing and wholly feeling, and hearing him spiritually and delectably smelling him and sweetly tasting him. And there we shall see God face to face, familiarly and wholly. The creature which is made will see and endlessly contemplate God who is the maker; for so can no man see God and live afterwards, that is to say in this mortal life. But when he of his special grace wishes to show himself here, he gives the creature more than its own strength, and he measures the revelation according to his own will, and it is profitable for that time.

"But our good Lord the Holy Spirit, who is endless life dwelling in our soul, protects us most faithfully and produces in the soul a peace, and brings it to ease through grace, and makes it obedient and reconciles it to God."

There are two particular debts which our soul has to pay. One is that we reverently marvel; the other is that we meekly suffer, always rejoicing in God. For he wants us to know that in a short time we shall see clearly in him all that we desire. And notwithstanding all this, I contemplated and wondered greatly what is the mercy and forgiveness of God; for by the teaching which I had before, I understood that the mercy of God will be remission of his wrath after we have sinned. For it seemed to me that to a soul whose intention and desire is to love, God's wrath would be harder than any other pain. And therefore I accepted that the remission of his wrath would be one of the chief characteristics of his mercy. But for anything which I could see or desire, I could not see this characteristic in all the revelation. But I shall describe something of how I saw and understood the operation of mercy, as God will give me grace.

I understood in this way. Man is changeable in this life, and falls into sin through naivete and ignorance. He is weak and foolish in himself, and also his will is overpowered in the time when he is assailed and in sorrow and woe. And the cause is blindness, because he does not see God; for if he saw God continually, he would have no harmful feelings nor any kind of prompting, no sorrowing which is conducive to sin.

So I saw and felt at the same time, and it seemed to me that the sight and the feeling were great and plentiful and gracious in comparison with what is our common feeling in this life. But still it seemed to me humble and petty in comparison with the great desire which the soul has to see God. For I felt in myself five kinds of activity, and they are these: rejoicing, mourning, desire, fear and true hope. Rejoicing, because God gave me knowledge and understanding that it was himself whom I saw. Mourning, and that was because of weakness. Desire, which was that I might see him always more and more; understanding and knowing that we shall never have perfect rest until we see him clearly and truly in heaven. The fear was because it seemed to me in all that time that that sight would fail and I should be left to myself. The true hope was in the endless love, for I saw that I should be protected by his mercy and brought to bliss.

And the rejoicing in his sight with this true hope of his merciful protection made me have feeling and comfort, so that the mourning and fear were not very painful. And still in all this I contemplated in this revelation by God that this kind of vision of him cannot persist in this life, and that is for his own glory and for the increase of our endless joy. And therefore often we fail to perceive him, and presently we fall back upon ourselves, and then we find that we feel nothing at all but the opposition that is in ourselves, and that comes from the old root of our first sin, with all that follows from our own persistence; and in this we are belaboured and tempted with the feeling of sin and of pain in many different ways, spiritually and bodily, as is known to us in this life.

But our good Lord the Holy Spirit, who is endless life dwelling in our soul, protects us most faithfully and produces in the soul a peace, and brings it to ease through grace, and makes it obedient and reconciles it to God. And this is the mercy and the way on which our good Lord constantly leads us, so long as we are in this changeable life. For I saw no wrath except on man's side, and he forgives that in us, for wrath is nothing else but a perversity and an opposition to peace and to love. And it comes from a lack of power or a lack of wisdom or a lack of goodness, and this lack is not in God, but it is on our side. For we through sin and wretchedness have in us a wrath and a constant opposition to peace and to love; and he revealed that very often in his lovely look of compassion and pity. For the foundation of mercy is in love, and the operation of mercy is our protection in love; and this was revealed in such a way that I could not perceive, about mercy's properties, in any other way than as if it were all love in love.

That is to say, as I see it, mercy is a sweet, gracious operation in love, mingled with plentiful pity, for mercy works, protecting us, and mercy works, turning everything to good for us. Mercy for love allows us to fail to a certain extent; and inasmuch as we fail, in so much we fall, and inasmuch as we fall, in so much we die. For we must necessarily die inasmuch as we fail to see and feel God, who is our life. Our failing is dreadful, our falling is shameful, and our dying is sorrowful. But yet in all this the sweet eye of pity is never turned away from us, and the operation of mercy does not cease.

For I contemplated the property of mercy, and I contemplated the property of grace, which have two ways of operating in one love. Mercy is a compassionate property, which belongs to motherhood in tender love; and grace is an honourable property, which belongs to royal dominion in the same love. Mercy works, protecting, enduring, vivifying and healing, and it is all of the tenderness of love; and grace works with mercy, raising, rewarding, endlessly exceeding what our love and labour deserve, distributing and displaying the vast plenty and generosity of God's royal dominion in his wonderful courtesy. And this is from the abundance of love, for grace transforms our dreadful failing into plentiful and endless solace; and grace transforms our shameful falling into high and honourable rising; and grace transforms our sorrowful dying into holy, blessed life.

For I saw most truly that always, as our contrariness makes for us here on earth pain, shame and sorrow, just so in contrary manner grace makes for us in heaven solace, honour and bliss, so superabundant that when we come up and receive that sweet reward which grace has made for us, there we shall thank and bless our Lord, endlessly rejoicing that we ever suffered woe; and that will be because of a property of the blessed love which we shall know in God, which we might never have known without woe preceding it. And when I saw all this, I was forced to agree that the mercy of God and his forgiveness abate and dispel our wrath.

For it was a great marvel, constantly shown to the soul in all the revelations, and the soul was contemplating with great diligence that our Lord God cannot in his own judgment forgive, because he cannot be angry—that would be impossible. For this was revealed, that our life is all founded and rooted in love, and without love we cannot live. And therefore to the soul which by God's special grace sees so much of his great and wonderful goodness as that we are endlessly united to him in love, it is the most impossible thing which could be that God might be angry, for anger and friendship are two contraries; for he dispels and destroys our wrath and makes us meek and mild—we must necessarily believe that he is always one in love, meek and mild, which is contrary to wrath. For I saw most truly that where our Lord appears, peace is received and wrath has no place; for I saw no kind of wrath in God, neither briefly nor for long. For truly, as I see it, if God could be angry for any time, we should neither have life nor place nor being; for as truly as we have our being from the endless power of God and from his endless wisdom and from his endless goodness, just as truly we have our preservation in the endless power of God and in his endless wisdom and in his endless goodness. For though we may feel in ourselves anger, contention and strife, still we are all mercifully enclosed in God's mildness and in his meekness, in his benignity and in his accessibility.

For I saw very truly that all our endless friendship, our place, our life and our being are in God. For that same endless goodness which protects us when we sin so that we do not perish, that same endless goodness constantly draws into us a peace, opposing our wrath and our perverse falling, and makes us see our need with true fear, and urgently to beseech God that we may have forgiveness, with a grace-given desire for our salvation. For we cannot be blessedly saved until we are truly in peace and in love, for that is our salvation.

And though we may be angry, and the contrariness which is in us be now in tribulation, distress and woe, as we fall victims to our blindness and our evil propensities, still we are sure and safe by God's merciful protection, so that we do not perish. But we are not blessedly safe, possessing our endless joy, until we are all in peace and in love, that is to say wholly contented with God and with all his works and with all his judgments, and loving and content with ourselves and with our fellow Christians and with everything which God loves, as is pleasing to love. And God's goodness does this in us.

So I saw that God is our true peace; and he is our safe protector when we ourselves are in disquiet, and he constantly works to bring us into endless peace. And so when by the operation of mercy and grace we are made meek and mild, then we are wholly safe. Suddenly the soul is united to God, when she is truly pacified in herself, for in him is found no wrath. And so I saw that when we are wholly in peace and in love, we find no contrariness in any kind of hindrance, and our Lord God in his goodness makes the contrariness which is in us now very profitable for us. For contrariness is the cause of all our tribulation and all our woe; and our Lord Jesus takes them and sends them up to heaven, and then they are made more sweet and delectable than heart can think or tongue can tell. And when we come there, we shall find them ready, all turned into true beauty and endless honour.

So is God our steadfast foundation, and he will be our whole joy, and he will make us as unchangeable as he is when we are there.

◆

"God is closer to us than our own soul, for he is the foundation on which our soul stands, and he is the means which keeps the substance and the sensuality together, so that they will never separate. For our soul sits in God in true rest, and our soul stands in God in sure strength, and our soul is naturally rooted in God in endless love."

And for the great endless love that God has for all mankind, he makes no distinction in love between the blessed soul of Christ and the least soul that will be saved. For it is very easy to believe and trust that the dwelling of the blessed soul of Christ is very high in the glorious divinity; and truly, as I understand our Lord to mean, where the blessed soul of Christ is, there is the substance of all the souls which will be saved by Christ.

Greatly ought we to rejoice that God dwells in our soul; and more greatly ought we to rejoice that our soul dwells in God. Our soul is created to be God's dwelling place, and the dwelling of our soul is God, who is uncreated. It is a great understanding to see and know inwardly that God, who is our Creator, dwells in our soul, and it is a far greater understanding to see and know inwardly that our soul, which is created, dwells in God in substance, of which substance, through God, we are what we are.

And I saw no difference between God and our substance, but, as it were, all God; and still my understanding accepted that our substance is in God, that is to say that God is God, and our substance is a creature in God. For the almighty truth of the Trinity is our Father, for he made us and keeps us in him. And the deep wisdom of the Trinity is our Mother, in whom we are enclosed. And the high goodness of the Trinity is our Lord, and in him we are enclosed and he in us. We are enclosed in the Father, and we are enclosed in the Son, and we are enclosed in the Holy Spirit. And the Father is enclosed in us, the Son is enclosed in us, and the Holy Spirit is enclosed in us, almighty, all wisdom and all goodness, one God, one Lord. And our faith is a power which comes from our natural substance into our sensual soul by the Holy Spirit, in which power all our powers come to us, for without that no man can receive power, for it is nothing else than right understanding with true belief and certain trust in our being, that we are in God and he in us, which we do not see.

And this power with all the others which God has ordained for us, entering there, works great things in us; for Christ is mercifully working in us, and we are by grace according with him, through the gift and the power of the Holy Spirit. This working makes it so that we are Christ's children and live Christian lives.

And so Christ is our way, safely leading us in his laws, and Christ in his body mightily bears us up into heaven; for I saw that Christ, having us all in him who shall be saved by him, honourably presents his Father in heaven with us, which present his Father most thankfully receives, and courteously gives to his Son Jesus Christ. This gift and operation is joy to the Father and bliss to the Son and delight to the Holy Spirit, and of everything which is our duty, it is the greatest delight to our Lord that we rejoice in this joy which the blessed Trinity has over our salvation.

...and despite all our feelings of woe or of well-being, God wants us to understand and to believe that we are more truly in heaven than on earth. Our faith comes from the natural love of our soul, and from the clear light of our reason, and from the steadfast memory which we have from God in our first creation. And when our soul is breathed into our body, at which time we are made sensual, at once mercy and grace begin to work, having care of us and protecting us with pity and love, in which operation the Holy Spirit forms in our faith the hope that we shall return up above to our substance, into the power of Christ, increased and fulfilled through the Holy Spirit. So I understood that our sensuality is founded in nature, in mercy and in grace, and this foundation enables us to receive gifts which lead us to endless life. For I saw very surely that our substance is in God, and I also saw that God is in our sensuality, for in the same instant and place in which our soul is made sensual, in that same instant and place exists the city of God, ordained for him from without beginning. He comes into this city and will never depart from it, for God is never out of the soul, in which he will dwell blessedly without end.

...And all the gifts which God can give to the creature he has given to his Son Jesus for us, which gifts he, dwelling in us, has enclosed in him until the time that we are fully grown, our soul together with our body and our body together with our soul. Let either of them take help from the other, until we have grown to full stature as creative nature brings about; and then in the foundation of creative nature with the operation of mercy, the Holy Spirit by grace breathes into us gifts leading to endless life.

And so my understanding was led by God to see in him and to know, to understand and to recognize that our soul is a created trinity, like the uncreated blessed Trinity, known and loved from without beginning, and in the creation united to the Creator, as is said before. This sight was sweet and wonderful to contemplate, peaceful and restful, secure and delectable. And because of the glorious union which was thus made by God between the soul and the body, mankind had necessarily to be restored from a double death, which restoration could never be until the time when the second person in the Trinity had taken the lower part of human nature, whose highest part was united to him in its first creation. And these two parts were in Christ, the higher and the lower, which are only one soul. The higher part was always at peace with God in full joy and bliss. The lower part, which is sensuality, suffered for the salvation of mankind....

And so I saw most surely that it is quicker for us and easier to come to the knowledge of God than it is to know our own soul. For our soul is so deeply grounded in God and so endlessly treasured that we cannot come to knowledge of it until we first have knowledge of God, who is the Creator to whom it is united. But nevertheless I saw that we have, naturally from our fulness, to desire wisely and truly to know our own soul, through which we are taught to seek it where it is, and that is in God. And so by the leading through grace of the Holy Spirit we shall know them both in one; whether we are moved to know God or our soul, either motion is good and true. God is closer to us than our own soul, for he is the foundation on which our soul stands, and he is the mean which keeps the substance and the sensuality together, so that they will never separate. For our soul sits in God in true rest, and our soul stands in God in sure strength, and our soul is naturally rooted in God in endless love. And therefore if we want to have knowledge of our soul, and communion and discourse with it, we must seek in our Lord God in whom it is enclosed.

And...as regards our substance, it can rightly be called our soul, and as regards our sensuality, it can rightly be called our soul, and that is by the union which it has in God.

That honourable city in which our Lord Jesus sits is our sensuality, in which he is enclosed; and our natural substance is enclosed in Jesus, with the blessed soul of Christ sitting in rest in the divinity. And I saw very certainly that we must necessarily be in longing and in penance until the time when we are led so deeply into God that we verily and truly know our own soul; and I saw certainly that our good Lord himself leads us into this high depth, in the same love with which he created us and in the same love with which he redeemed us, by mercy and grace, through the power of his blessed Passion.

And all this notwithstanding, we can never come to the full knowledge of God until we first clearly know our own soul. For until the time that it is in its full powers, we cannot be all holy; and that is when our sensuality by the power of Christ's Passion can be brought up into the substance, with all the profits of our tribulation which our Lord will make us obtain through mercy and grace.

I had a partial touching, and it is founded in nature, that is to say: Our reason is founded in God, who is nature's substance. From this substantial nature spring mercy and grace, and penetrate us, accomplishing everything for the fulfillment of our joy. These are our foundations, in which we have our being, our increase and our fulfillment. For in nature we have our life and our being, and in mercy and grace we have our increase and our fulfillment. This is three properties in one goodness, and where one operates all operate in the things which now pertain to us.

God wants us to understand, desiring with all our heart and all our strength to have knowledge of them, always more and more until the time that we are fulfilled; for to know them fully and to see them clearly is nothing else than endless joy and bliss, which we shall have in heaven, which God wants us to begin here in knowledge of his love. For we cannot profit by our reason alone, unless we have equally memory and love; nor can we be saved merely because we have in God our natural foundation, unless we have, coming from the same foundation, mercy and grace. For from these three operating all together we receive all our good, the first of which is the good of nature. For in our first making God gave us as much good and as great good as we could receive in our spirit alone; but his prescient purpose in his endless wisdom willed that we should be double.

And as regards our substance, he made us so noble and so rich that always we achieve his will and his glory. When I say 'we,' that means men who will be saved. For truly I saw that we are that which he loves, and that we do what is pleasing to him, constantly, without any stinting. And from this great richness and this high nobility, commensurate powers come into our soul, whilst it is joined to our body, in which joining we are made sensual. And so in our substance we are full and in our sensuality we are lacking, and this lack God will restore and fill by the operation of mercy and grace, plentifully flowing into us from his own natural goodness. And so this natural goodness makes mercy and grace to work in us, and the natural goodness that we have from him enables us to receive the operation of mercy and grace.

I saw that our nature is wholly in God, in which he makes diversities flowing out of him to perform his will, which nature preserves and mercy and grace restore and fulfil. And of these none will be destroyed, for our nature, which is the higher part, is joined to God in its creation, and God is joined to our nature, which is the lower part in taking flesh. And so in Christ our two natures are united, for the Trinity is comprehended in Christ, in whom our higher part is founded and rooted; and our lower part the second person has taken, which nature was first prepared for him....

FROM THE SIXTEENTH REVELATION

"The place which Jesus takes in our soul he will nevermore vacate, for in us is his home of homes and his everlasting dwelling."

And then our good Lord opened my spiritual eye, and showed me my soul in the midst of my heart. I saw the soul as wide as if it were an endless citadel, and also as if it were a blessed kingdom, and from the state which I saw in it, I understood that it is a fine city. In the midst of that city sits our Lord Jesus, true God and true man, a handsome person and tall, highest bishop, most awesome king, most honourable lord. And I saw him splendidly clad in honours. He sits erect there in the soul, in peace and rest, and he rules and guards heaven and earth and everything that is. The humanity and the divinity sit at rest, the divinity rules and guards, without instrument or effort. And the soul is wholly occupied by the blessed divinity, sovereign power, sovereign wisdom and sovereign goodness.

The place which Jesus takes in our soul he will nevermore vacate, for in us is his home of homes and his everlasting dwelling. An in this he revealed the delight that he has in the creation of man's soul; for as well as the Father could create a creature and as well as the Son could create a creature, so well did the Holy Spirit want man's spirit to be created, and so it was done. And therefore the blessed Trinity rejoices without end in the creation of man's soul, for it saw without beginning what would delight it without end.

Everything which God has made shows his dominion, as understanding was given at the same time by the example of a creature who is led to see the great nobility and the rulership which is fitting to a lord, and when it had seen all the nobility beneath, then in wonder it was moved to seek up above for that high place where the lord dwells, knowing by reason that his dwelling is in the most honourable place. And thus I understood truly that our soul may never have rest in anything which is beneath itself. And when it comes above all creatures into itself, still it cannot remain contemplating itself; but all its contemplation is blessedly set in God, who is the Creator, dwelling there, for in man's soul is his true dwelling.

And the greatest light and the brightest shining in the city is the glorious love of our Lord God, as I see it. And what can make us to rejoice more in God than to see in him that in us, of all his greatest works, he has joy? For I saw in the same revelation that if the blessed Trinity could have created man's soul any better, any fairer, any nobler than it was created, the Trinity would not have been fully pleased with the creation of man's soul. But because it made man's soul as beautiful, as good, as precious a creature as it could make, therefore the blessed Trinity is fully pleased without end in the creation of man's soul. And it wants our hearts to be powerfully lifted above the depths of the earth and all empty sorrows, and to rejoice in it.

♦

"So I saw how sin is for a short time deadly to the blessed creatures of endless life, and always, the more clearly that the soul sees the blessed face by the grace of loving, the more it longs to see it in fulness, that is to say in God's own likeness."

But now I must tell how I saw that sin is deadly in creatures who will not die for sin but live in the joy of God without end. I saw that two opposites ought not to be together in one place. The two greatest oppositions which exist are the highest bliss and the deepest pain. The highest bliss there is, is to possess God in the clarity of endless light, truly seeing him, sweetly feeling him, peacefully possessing him in the fulness of joy; and a part of this blessed aspect of our Lord God was revealed. In this revelation I saw that sin was the greatest opposition to this, so much so that as long as we have anything to do with any kind of sin, we shall never clearly see the blessed face of God. And the more horrible and grievous our sins may be, the deeper are we for that time fallen from this blessed sight.

And therefore it often seems to us as if we were in danger of death and in some part of hell, because of the sorrow and the pain which sin is to us, and so for that time we are dead to the true sight of our blessed life. But in all this I saw truly that we are not dead in the sight of God, nor does he ever depart from us; but he will never have his full joy in us until we have our full joy in him, truly seeing his fair, blessed face. For we are ordained to this by nature, and brought to it by grace.

So I saw how sin is for a short time deadly to the blessed creatures of endless life, and always, the more clearly that the soul sees the blessed face by the grace of loving, the more it longs to see it in fulness, that is to say in God's own likeness. For even though our Lord God dwells now in us, and is here with us, and embraces us and encloses us for his tender love, so that he can never leave us, and is nearer to us than tongue can tell or heart can think, still we can never cease from mourning and weeping, seeking and longing, until we see him clearly, face to his blessed face, for in that precious sight no woe can remain, no well-being can be lacking.

And in this I saw matter for mirth and matter for mourning—matter for mirth, that our Lord, our maker is so near to us and in us, and we in him, because of his great goodness he keeps us faithfully; matter for mourning, because our spiritual eye is so blind, and we are so burdened with the weight of our mortal flesh and the darkness of sin that we cannot see clearly the blessed face of our Lord God. No, and because of this darkness, we can scarcely believe or have faith in this great love and his faithfulness, with which he protects us. And so it is that I say that we can never cease mourning and weeping.

This weeping does not only mean the outpouring of tears from our mortal eyes, but it has a more spiritual understanding; for the natural desire of our soul is so great and so immeasurable that if all the nobility which God ever created in heaven and on earth were given to us for our joy and our comfort, if we did not see his own fair blessed face, still we should never cease to mourn and to weep in the spirit, because, that is, of our painful longing, until we might see our Creator's fair blessed face. And if we were in all the pain that heart can think or tongue can tell, if we could at that time see his blessed face, all this pain would not grieve us.

So is that blessed vision the end of every kind of pain to loving souls, and the fulfillment of every kind of joy and bliss; and that he revealed in the great, marvelous words when he says: I am he who is highest, I am he whom you love, I am he who is all.

We ought to have three kinds of knowledge. The first is that we know our Lord God. The second is that we know ourselves, what we are through him in nature and in grace. The third is that we know humbly that our self is opposed to our sin and to our weakness. And all this revelation was made, as I understand it, for these three.

♦

"But I know well that our Lord revealed to me no souls but those who fear him, for I know well that the soul which truly accepts the teaching of the Holy Spirit hates sin more, for its vileness and horribleness, than it does all the pain which is in hell."

I saw that God can do everything which is necessary for us; and these three necessities which I shall describe compel us to long in love. Pity and love protect us in the time of our need; and the longing in the same love draws us into heaven, for God's thirst is to have man, generally, drawn into him, and in that thirst he has drawn his holy souls who are now in bliss. And so, getting his living members, always he draws and drinks, and still he thirsts and he longs.

I saw three kinds of longing in God, and all to the same end, and we have the same in us, and from the same power, and for the same end. The first is because he longs to teach us to know him and to love him always more and more, as is suitable and profitable to us. The second is that he longs to bring us up into bliss, as souls are when they are taken out of pain into heaven. The third is to fill us with bliss, and that will be fulfilled on the last day, to last forever. For I saw what is known in our faith, that pain and sorrow will be ended then for those who will be saved. And not only shall we receive the same bliss which souls have had already in heaven, but also we shall receive a new bliss, which will be plenteously flowing out of God into us, and will fill us full.

And those are the good things which he has ordained from without beginning to give us. These good things are treasured and hidden in himself, for until that time, the creature has not the power or merit to receive them. In this we should truly see the cause of all the deeds which God has done; and furthermore, we should see the cause of all the things which he has permitted; and the bliss and the fulfillment will be so deep and so high that, out of wonder and marvelling, all creatures ought to have for God so much reverent fear, surpassing what has been seen and felt before, that the pillars of heaven will tremble and quake.

But this kind of trembling and fear will have no kind of pain, but it is proper to God's honourable majesty so to be contemplated by his creatures, trembling and quaking in fear, because of their much greater joy endlessly marvelling at the greatness of God, the Creator, and at the smallest part of all that is created.

For the contemplation of this makes the creature marvelously meek and mild; and therefore God wants us, and it is also proper to us, both by nature and by grace, to want to have knowledge of this, desiring the vision and the action. For it leads us in the right way, and keeps us in true life, and unites us to God.

And as good as God is, so great is he; and as much as it is proper to his divinity to be loved, so much is it proper to his great exaltedness to be feared. For this reverent fear is the fairer courtesy which is in heaven before God's face; and by as much as he will be known and loved, surpassing how he now is, by so much will he be feared, surpassing how he now is. Therefore it must necessarily be that all heaven, all earth will tremble and quake when the pillars will tremble and quake.

I say very little about this reverent fear, for I hope that it may be seen in what has been said before. But I know well that our Lord revealed to me no souls but those who fear him, for I know well that the soul which truly accepts the teaching of the Holy Spirit hates sin more, for its vileness and horribleness, than it does all the pain which is in hell. For the soul which contemplates the gentleness of Jesus does not hate any hell, but the sin of hell, as I see it. And therefore it is

God's will that we recognize sin, and pray busily and labour willingly and seek meekly for teaching, so that we do not fall blindly into it, and if we fall, so that we quickly rise. For the greatest pain that the soul can have is at any time to turn from God through sin.

The soul which wants to be in rest should, when other men's sins come to mind, flee that as the pain of hell, seeking from God help against it. For the contemplation of other men's sins makes as it were a thick mist before the soul's eye, and during that time we cannot see the beauty of God, unless we can contemplate them [that is, a man's sins] with contrition with him [that is, the sinner], with compassion on him, and with holy desires to God for him. For without this it harasses and troubles and hinders the soul which contemplates them....

♦

"...for it is a most lovely humility in a sinful soul, made by the mercy and grace of the Holy Spirit, when we are willing and glad to accept the scourging and chastising which our Lord himself wishes to give us. And it will be very tender and very easy, if

we will only keep ourselves content with him and with all his works."

Our good Lord showed the fiend's enmity, by which I understood that everything which is opposed to love and to peace is from the fiend and from his side. We are liable through our feebleness and our folly to fall, and we are able through the mercy and the grace of the Holy Spirit to rise to greater joy. And if our enemy gains anything from us by our falling, which is his delight, he loses many times more in our rising by our charity and our meekness; and this glorious rising is to him such great sorrow and pain, because of the hatred which he has for our souls, that he burns constantly in envy. And all this sorrow which he would make us have will come back to him, and this was why our Lord scorned him, and revealed that he will be scorned; and this made me to laugh greatly.

So this is the remedy, that we acknowledge our wretchedness and flee to our Lord; for always, the more abased we are, the more profitable it is for us to touch him. And let us then in intention say this: I know well that I have deserved pain; but our Lord is almighty, and may punish me greatly, and he is all wisdom, and can punish me wisely, and he is all goodness, and loves me tenderly. And it is profitable for us to remain in this contemplation; for it is a most lovely humility in a sinful soul, made by the mercy and grace of the Holy Spirit, when we are willing and glad to accept the scourging and the chastising which our Lord himself wishes to give us. And it will be very tender and very easy, if we will only keep ourselves content with him and with all his works.

As to the penance which one takes upon oneself, that was not revealed to me; that is to say, it was not revealed to me specifically. But what was revealed, specially and greatly and in a most loving manner, is that we ought meekly and patiently to bear and suffer the penance which God himself gives us, with recollection of his blessed Passion. For when we recall his blessed Passion, with pity and love, then we suffer with him as his friends did who saw it....

For he says: Do not accuse yourself that your tribulation and your woe is all your fault; for I do not want you to be immoderately depressed or sorrowful. For I tell you that whatever you do, you will have woe. And therefore I want you wisely to understand the penance which you are continually in, and to accept that meekly for your penance. And then you will truly see that all your life is profitable penance.

This place is prison, this life is penance, and he wants us to rejoice in the remedy.

The remedy is that our Lord is with us, protecting us and leading us into the fulness of joy; for our Lord intends this to be an endless joy, that he who will be our bliss when we are there is our protector whilst we are here, our way and our heaven in true love and faithful trust....

Let us flee to our Lord, and we shall be comforted. Let us touch him, and we shall be made clean. Let us cleave to him, and we shall be sure and safe from every kind of peril. For our courteous Lord wants us to be as familiar with him as heart may think or soul may desire; but let us beware that we do not accept this familiarity so carelessly as to forsake courtesy. For our Lord himself is supreme familiarity, and he is as courteous as he is familiar, for he is true courtesy. And he wants to have the blessed creatures who will be in heaven with him without end like himself in all things, and to be perfectly like our Lord is our true salvation and our greatest bliss. And if we do not know how we shall do all this, let us desire it from our Lord, and he will teach us, for that is his own delight and his glory, blessed may he be.

Our Lord in his mercy reveals our sin and our feebleness to us by the sweet gracious light of his own self, for our sin is so foul and so horrible that he in his courtesy will not reveal it to us except by the light of his mercy.

It is his will that we have knowledge of four things. The first is that he is the foundation from whom we have our life and our being. The second is that he protects us mightily and mercifully, during the time that we are in our sin, among all our enemies who are so fierce against us; and we are in so much more peril because we give them occasion for this, and we do not know our own need. The third is how courteously he protects us and makes us know that we are going astray. The fourth is how steadfastly he waits for us, and does not change his demeanour, for he wants us to be converted and united to him in love, as he is to us.

And so by knowledge and grace we may see our sin, profitably, without despair. For truly we need to see it, and by the sight we should be made ashamed of ourselves, and broken down from our pride and our presumption. For truly it behooves us to see that in

ourselves we are nothing at all but sin and wretchedness. And so by the sight of the less which our Lord
reveals to us, the more which we do not see is dis-
pelled. For he in his courtesy measures the sight for us;
for it so foul and so horrible that we should not endure
to see it as it is.

And so by this meek knowledge, through contrition
and grace we shall be broken down from everything
which is not our Lord. And then will our blessed saviour cure us perfectly and unite us to him. This break-
ing and this curing our Lord intends for men in
general, for he who is highest and closest to God may
see himself sinful and needy along with me. And I
who am the least and the lowest of those who will be
saved may be comforted along with him who is highest. So has our Lord united us in charity.

When he revealed to me that I should sin, what for
the joy that I had in contemplating him, I did not
attend promptly to that revelation, and so our courteous Lord paused there, and did not wish to teach me
any more until he had given me the grace and will to
attend. And by this I was taught that though we may be
lifted up high into contemplation by the special gift of
our Lord, still, together with this, we must necessarily

have knowledge and sight of our sin and of our feebleness; for without this knowledge we may not have true meekness, and without this we cannot be safe. And I also saw that we cannot have this knowledge through ourselves or through any of our spiritual enemies, for they do not wish so much good to us. For if it were according to their will, we should never see it until our last day. Then are we much indebted to God, who is willing himself for love to show it to us, in the time of mercy and of grace.

...And also in the same revelation, where I saw that I should sin, I was taught to be fearful because of my own uncertainty, because I do not know how I may fall, nor do I know the measure or the greatness of my sin. For in my fearfulness I wanted to know that, and I had no answer to it.

Also at that same time our courteous Lord revealed, most sweetly and most powerfully, the endlessness and the unchangeability of his love, and also his great goodness and his gracious protection of our spirit, so that the love between him and our souls will never be parted into eternity. And so in the fear I have matter for meekness, which saves me from presumption, and in the blessed revelation of love I have matter for true comfort and for joy, which saves me from despair.

All this familiar revelation of our courteous Lord is a lesson of love and a sweet, gracious teaching from himself, in comforting of our soul. For he wants us to know by the sweetness of his familiar love that all which we see or feel, within or without, which is in opposition to this is from the enemy and not from God, and in this way. If we are moved to be more careless about our way of life or about the custody of our heart, because we have knowledge of this plentiful love, then we have great need to beware of this impulse, should it come. It is false, and we ought to hate it greatly, for it has no resemblance to God's will. And when we have fallen through weakness or blindness, then our courteous Lord, touching us, moves us and protects us. And then he wants us to see our wretchedness and meekly to acknowledge it; but he does not want us to remain there, or to be much occupied in self-accusation, nor does he want us to be too full of our own misery. But he wants us quickly to attend to him, for he stands all alone, and he waits for us continually, moaning and mourning until we come. And he hastens to bring us to him for we are his joy and his delight, and he is the remedy of our life....

◆

"...and when we fall into sin, and neglect recollection of him and the protection of our own soul, then Christ bears all alone the burden of us."

Man endures in this life by three things, by which three God is honoured and we are furthered, protected and saved. The first is the use of man's natural reason. The second is the common teaching of Holy Church. The third is the inward grace-giving operation of the Holy spirit; and these three are all from one God. God is the foundation of our natural reason; and God is the teaching of Holy Church, and God is the Holy Spirit, and they are all different gifts, and he wants us to have great regard for them, and to accord ourselves to them. For they work continually in us, all together, and those are great things; and of this greatness he wants us to have knowledge here, as it were in an ABC. That is to say that we can have a little knowledge of that of which we shall have the fulness in heaven, and that is to further us.

We know in our faith that God alone took our

nature, and no one but he, and, furthermore, that Christ alone performed all the great works which belong to our salvation, and no one but he; and just so, he alone acts now in the last end, that is to say he dwells here in us, and rules us, and cares for us in this life, and brings us to his bliss. And so he will do as long as any soul is on earth who will come to heaven; and so much so that if there were no such soul on earth except one, he would be with it, all alone, until he had brought it up into his bliss.

I believe and understand the ministration of holy angels, as scholars tell, but it was not revealed to me; for God himself is nearest and meekest, highest and lowest, and he does everything, and not only all that we need, but also he does everything which is honourable for our joy in heaven; and when I say that he waits for us, moaning and mourning, that means all the true feelings which we have in ourselves, in contrition and in compassion, and all the moaning and mourning because we are not united with our Lord. And as such is profitable, it is Christ in us; and though some of us feel it seldom, it never leaves Christ until the time when he has brought us out of all our woe.

For love never allows him to be without pity; and

when we fall into sin, and neglect recollection of him and the protection of our own soul, then Christ bears all alone the burden of us. And so he remains, moaning and mourning. Then it is for us in reverence and kindness to turn quickly to our Lord, and not to leave him alone. He is here alone with us all; that is to say, he is here only for us. And when I am distant towards him through sin, despair or sloth, then I leave my Lord to remain alone, inasmuch as he is in me. And this is the case with us all who are sinners; but though it may be that we act like this often, his goodness never allows us to be alone, but constantly he is with us, and tenderly he excuses us, and always protects us from blame in his sight.

Our good Lord revealed himself to his creature in various ways, both in heaven and on earth; but I saw him take no place except in man's soul. He revealed himself on earth in the sweet Incarnation and his blessed Passion, and he showed himself in other ways on earth, where I said that I saw God in an instant of time; and he showed himself in another way on earth, as if it were on pilgrimage, that is to say that he is here with us, leading us, and will be until he has brought us all to his bliss in heaven.

He revealed himself several times reigning,...but principally in man's soul; he has taken there his resting place and his honourable city. Out of this honourable throne he will never rise or depart without end. Marvelous and splendid is the place where the Lord dwells; and therefore he wants us promptly to attend to the touching of his grace, rejoicing more in his unbroken love than sorrowing over our frequent fallings.

For it is the greatest glory to him of anything which we can do that we live gladly and happily for love of him in our penance. For he regards us so tenderly that he sees all our life here to be penance; for the substantial and natural longing in us for him is a lasting penance in us, and he makes this penance in us, and mercifully he helps us to bear it. For his love makes him long, his wisdom and his truth with his justice make him to suffer us here, and he wants to see this in us in this way. For this is our loving penance, and the greatest, as I see it, for this penance never leaves us until the time when we are fulfilled, when we shall have him for our reward.

And therefore he wants us to set our hearts on our passing over, that is to say from the pain which we feel to the bliss which we trust.

But here our courteous Lord revealed the moaning and the mourning of our soul, with this meaning: I know well that you wish to live for my love, joyfully and gladly suffering all the penance which may come to you; but since you do not live without sin, you are depressed and sorrowful, and if you could live without sin, you would suffer for my love all the woe which might come to you, and it is true. But do not be too much aggrieved by the sin which comes to you against your will.

And here I understood that the lord looked on the servant with pity and not with blame; for this passing life does not require us to live wholly without sin. He loves us endlessly, and we sin customarily, and he reveals it to us most gently. And then we sorrow and moan discreetly, turning to contemplate his mercy, cleaving to his love and to his goodness, seeing that his is our medicine, knowing that we only sin.

And so by the meekness which we obtain in seeing our sin, faithfully recognizing his everlasting love, thanking him and praising him, we please him. I love you and you love me, and our love will never be divided in two; and it is for your profit that I suffer.

SUGGESTIONS FOR FURTHER READING

1. *Julian of Norwich: Showings*, translated from the critical text with an introduction by Edmund Colledge, O.S.A., and James Walsh, S.J. (Classics of Western Spirituality Series. New York/Ramsey, N.J.: Paulist Press, 1978).

2. *Julian of Norwich: Reflections on Selected Texts* by Austin Cooper (Mystic, Conn.: Twenty Third Publications, 1988).

3. *Julian of Norwich's Showings: From Vision to Book* by Denise B. Baker (Princeton, N.J.: Princeton University Press, 1994).

OTHER BOOKS IN THE SERIES

TRUE JOY:
THE WISDOM OF FRANCIS AND CLARE

EVERYTHING AS DIVINE:
THE WISDOM OF MEISTER ECKHART

CREATION AND CHRIST:
THE WISDOM OF HILDEGARD OF BINGEN